THIS MONTH

- 5   CAN THE LATEST TECHNOLOGY REDUCE FASHION'S OVERSTOCKING PROBLEM?
- 8   FIRST DAY
- 11   2030
- 13   I SEE
- 15   THE EARTH WILL NOT END WITH US.
- 19   ME, WE, AND THE BEES
- 21   UNCONDITIONAL LOVE
- 22   MOTHER NATURE
- 25   PIERDA PERDIDA
- 27   PORTRAIT OF THE SALTON SEA

EDITORIAL SHOOT
Photographer: Josephine Jael Jimenez
Model: Brianna Ibarra

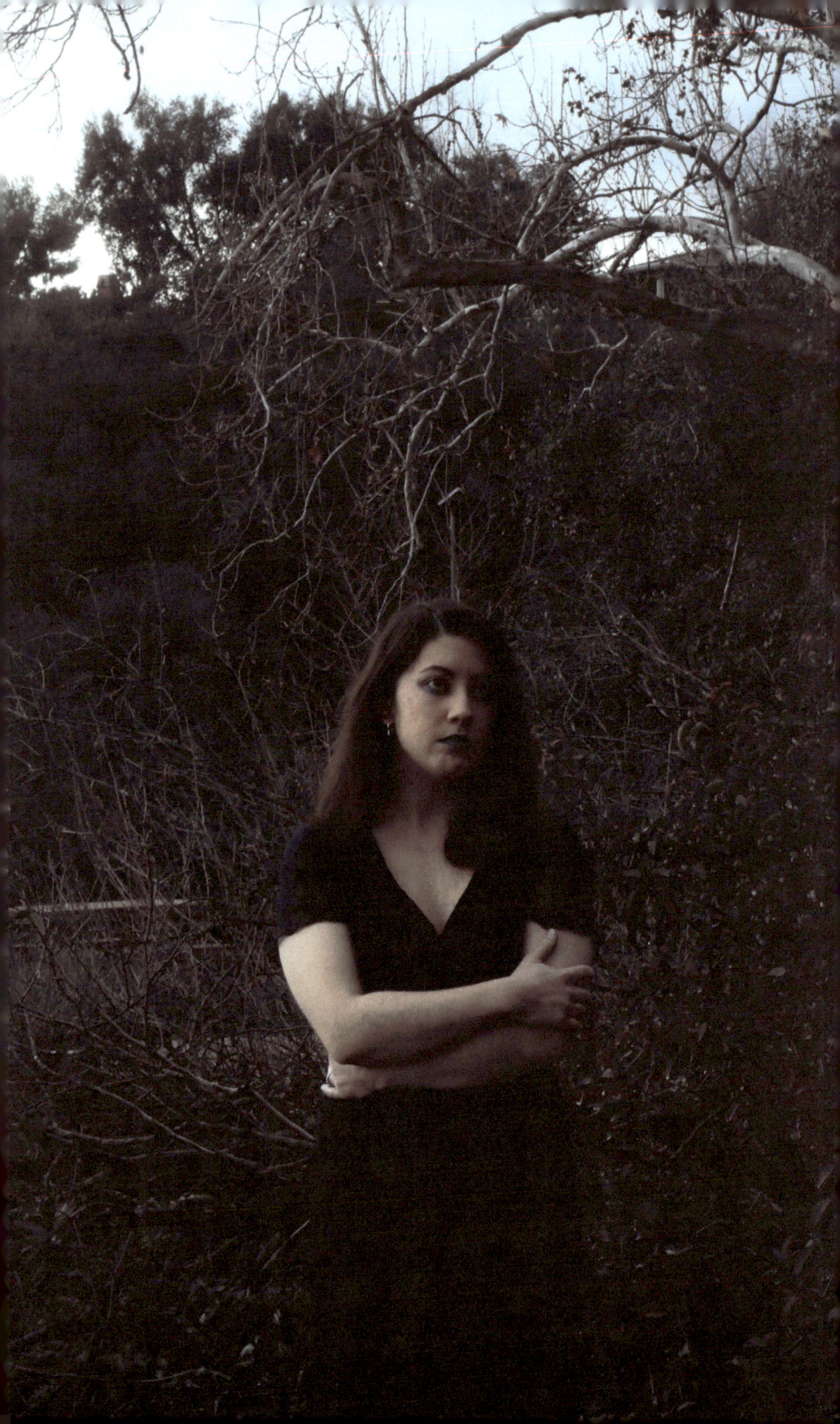

Can the latest technology reduce fashion's overstocking problem?

BRENDA HERNÁNDEZ JAIMES

The new technological advancements in the manufacturing sector could help you avoid garment overstock while reaping the benefits of a faster and more sustainable production process, but are these the ultimate solution?

With the rise of fast fashion, consumers have unlimited access to garments they see online and in stores, with mass retailers stocking excessive clothes and, manufacturers producing an absurd amount of overstock at the end of the season. While many brands sell overstock clothing to resale stores or donate to charities, others reportedly shred, burn or dump product in landfills. Such was the case for British luxury fashion house, Burberry, who throughout 2013-2018 burned unsold goods that ranged from clothes, perfume and accessories that were worth £28.6m in order to protect its brand. But why go through all that trouble, further polluting the environment which also ultimately hurts your bottom line?

Most consumers throw away 84% of unwanted clothing; it's not donated or re-sold, according to the Environmental Protection Agency. Americans collectively dispose of a total of 14 millions tons of clothing a year on average or 80 pounds per person. So It's essential to improve our ways of producing exactly what we need.

Placing importance on overstock reduction can help your brand maintain itself in the competitive sphere, save you money and make you a more responsible entrepreneur. Here are some of the latest technologies that are helping designers to build more with less:

The garment manufacturing process, from design to production, is divided into many different micro-operations managed by professionals who work together to create designs that are stylish, functional and profitable.

With the average number of Stock Keeping Units (SKU's) introduced by brands rising each season, keeping the communication smooth between teams becomes more difficult. If a system that helps streamline this data flow is not implemented, it's easy for clutter to accumulate.

For this reason, fashion teams are adopting for "smart collaboration" apps and platforms such as Google Sheets that allow multiple users to simultaneously interact and edit of a single file, like tech packs, for example. Also version control (also known as revision control and source control) like features allow all team-members to track doc changes and monitor team progress in general.

By having quick communications in real-time and the ability to instantly edit, and share tech packs with manufacturers help speed-up pace and efficiency of fashion developments. This way manufacturers too are able to facilitate cut-to-order for the brands and the later can too avoid minimum orders that primarily results in overstocking.

In order to establish a cohesive manufacturing process, a brand needs to have a clear creative direction. Most digitize their designs and artworks, utilizing software like Illustrator for flat sketches, or technologies like Kaledo for pattern making.

But, one of the latest and most interesting technologies to be coming our way is the 3D sample design like EFI's Optitex. It offers brands and manufactures quick solutions with their 3D model garment.

But how does this avoid overstock? This tech can help reduce the use of unnecessary fabrics, by presenting designers with a photorealistic 3D view model of their flat pattern design before they begin the cut and sew process.

3D designs that have custom made avatars provide a better image of how the style, fit and color of the garment will look like on your client before it's crafted. After perfecting your design with buttons, textile and stitching that you've envisioned, you can showcase your digital collection through your website and social media.

With this method, brands could now reduce rigorous and high-priced sampling process that also evades a costly and wasteful garment overstock.

Also making pre-ordering available has proved successful for many brands. Once your clients have paid for the garment that they saw on your online boutique or social media, your factory can begin to produce the quantity and sizes of your designs. Selecting a manufacturer that can provide you with

this option can ease your production and sale process.
Some designers are opting for what is known as micro-manufacturing or micro-factory. It's not only useful regarding supply chain speed, but also eliminates a lot of unnecessary costs and waste material, especially for a brand that is just starting out.
Microfactories are a great way to test the waters with potential clients before committing to full-scale production and avoid wastage of design and materials, and of course overstock. For instance, manufacturers like Good Clothing Company provide the lowest minimum order quantity in the production industry. With a garment order as low as 10 per color, size and style.
Some micro-factories also offer advanced technologies that make it possible to produce a complete collection in just a few days or weeks. Double printing stations, prototyping light machines and heaving fabrics to an automatic cut for a single sheet in sweaters or jeans, are some examples.
Everpress is another option for independent brands that can easily upload their designs through their campaign builder. They can choose through a wide selection of high-quality garments, retail price and profit margin. Through pre-orders, brands can easily view live sales statistics and any projected profits. At the end of the campaign, your purchased batch will be either screen printed or through Director To Garment (DTG) printing and shipped directly to your customers.
Still, whether you are working with a large manufacturer or a micro one, remember that communication between your teams and them is essential. It's essential to have every team member and your factory in the loop of the creation and design process. Clear communication will help avoid that divide which usually results in long product development cycles and errors that lead to waste and overstock.

1st day
1st finding my way
Embracing the in between
Language
Skin

Finding my people
Searching my people
Encuentro mi gente

Living the land
But also living me

Staying safe
But also staying free
Strange to have the night taken away from a night person

Missing the bustling life of the evening
But feeling closer to my humanity
When you wake up with the sun
and sleep with the moon
Your circadian rythym blooms

Decolonization is not easy
What you thought were things you loved
Were actually just vices like coca cola products fed to you
to make you think you like them
But really they are slowly killing your
Mind body and soul

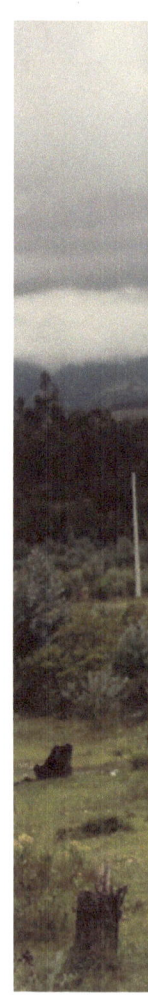

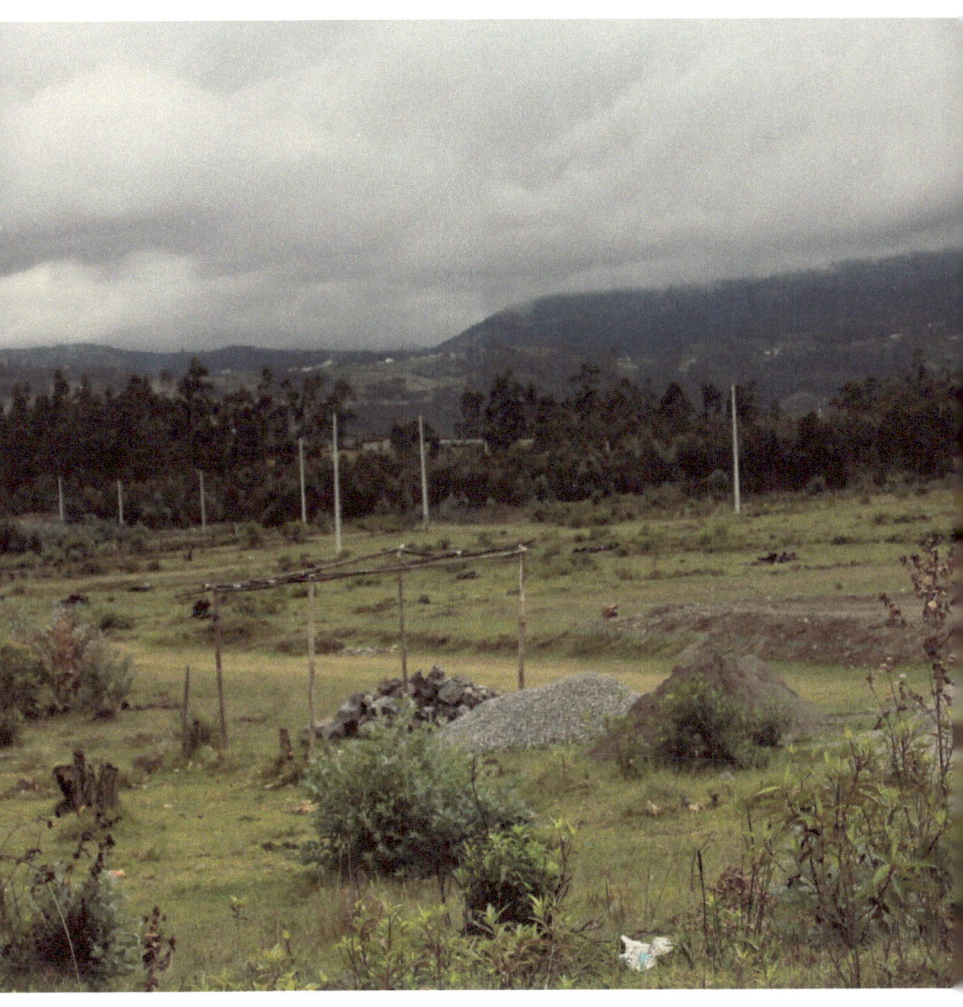

Photograph & Poem *by Yura Sapi*

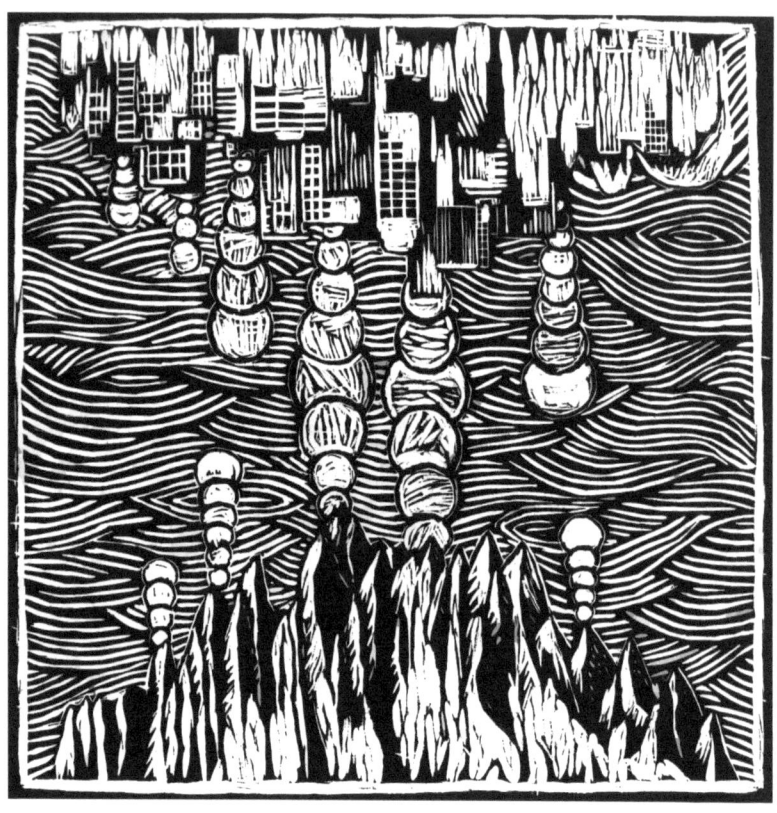

Sublime Sublimation
Relief Print *by Bekah Badilla*

2030

KELLY DUARTE

When sparks of apocalypse
consume the land in fire
will it burn a circle around your house
marking it safe?

Refugees in space
have viewing parties to see
swirling clouds close in on the world.
Do you think the hurricanes will spare you?

The money you have hidden on the drowning islands
buried in the erupting earth
carried in the melting bone
will death accept credit or debit?

The wilds will creep into the people
and the ouroboros of violence will reign
until the night is more welcoming than the light
What makes you so lucky to survive the blood?

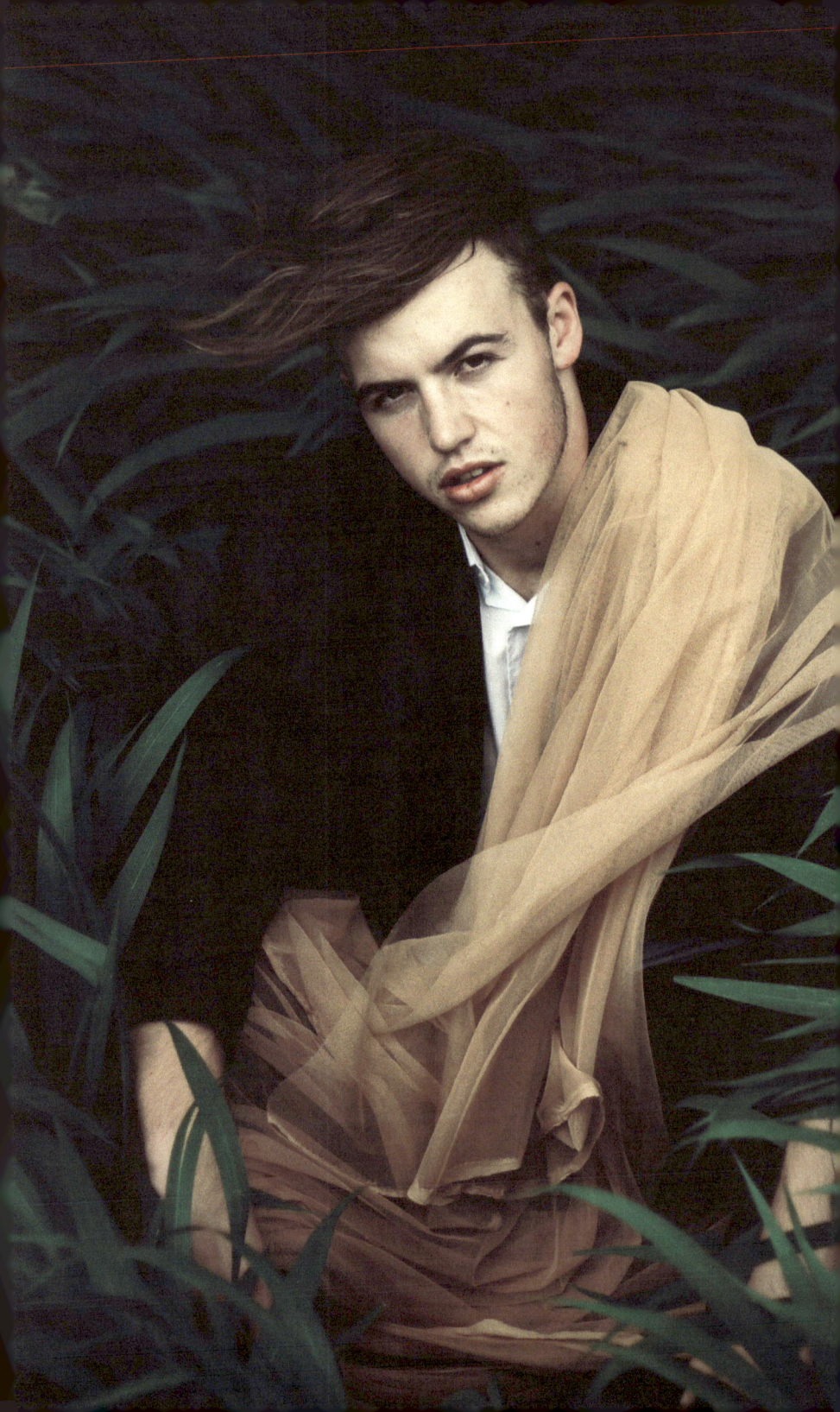

I SEE

JOSEPH A. REYES

Like a moth
To a flame
I couldn't resist the light

The brightness I saw was beautiful
The radiance of joy and childlikeness
Gave me permission
To be myself
To feel safe
To feel cared for
To feel like I could
Hold onto this light forever

Then...

The light was dim
The light was distant
The light was faint

I feel faint
I feel defensive
I feel resistant

I cannot let the light go out
It's my mission
It's my passion
It's my responsibility

But it isn't

The light does not know it exists
The light cannot see that it reveals its own path
The light is wandering

It'll see itself one day
I'll watch from afar and watch the light grow brighter and brighter

And maybe, one day, the light will enter my heart

But for now, the light must enter their heart again

I believe in us

Unveiled. The Series
Photograph *by Pierre Van Vuuren*

inhale dust to remember where you're going, just like everyone else.

Above: Graphic *by Josephine Jael Jimenez*
Right: Illustration *by Carri*

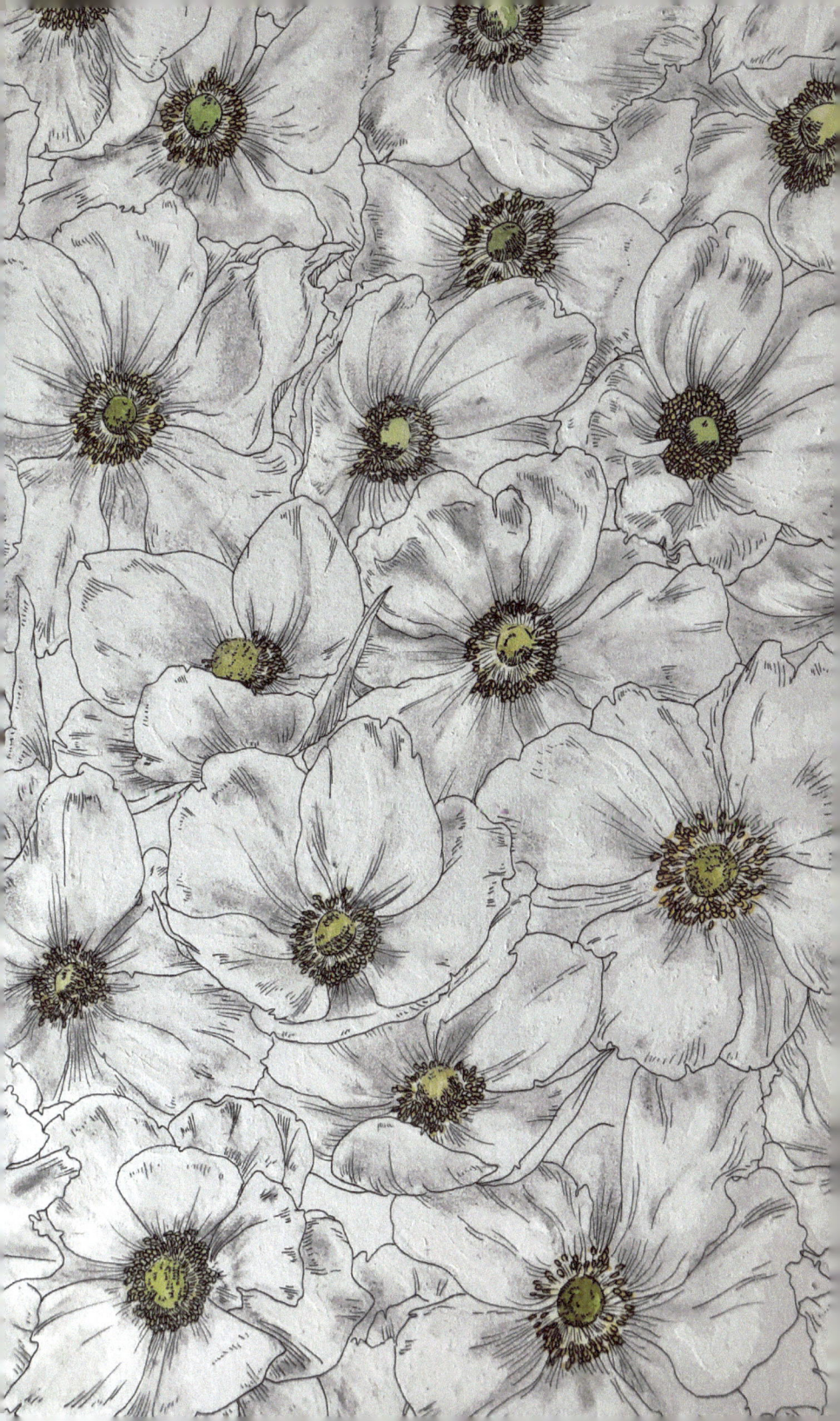

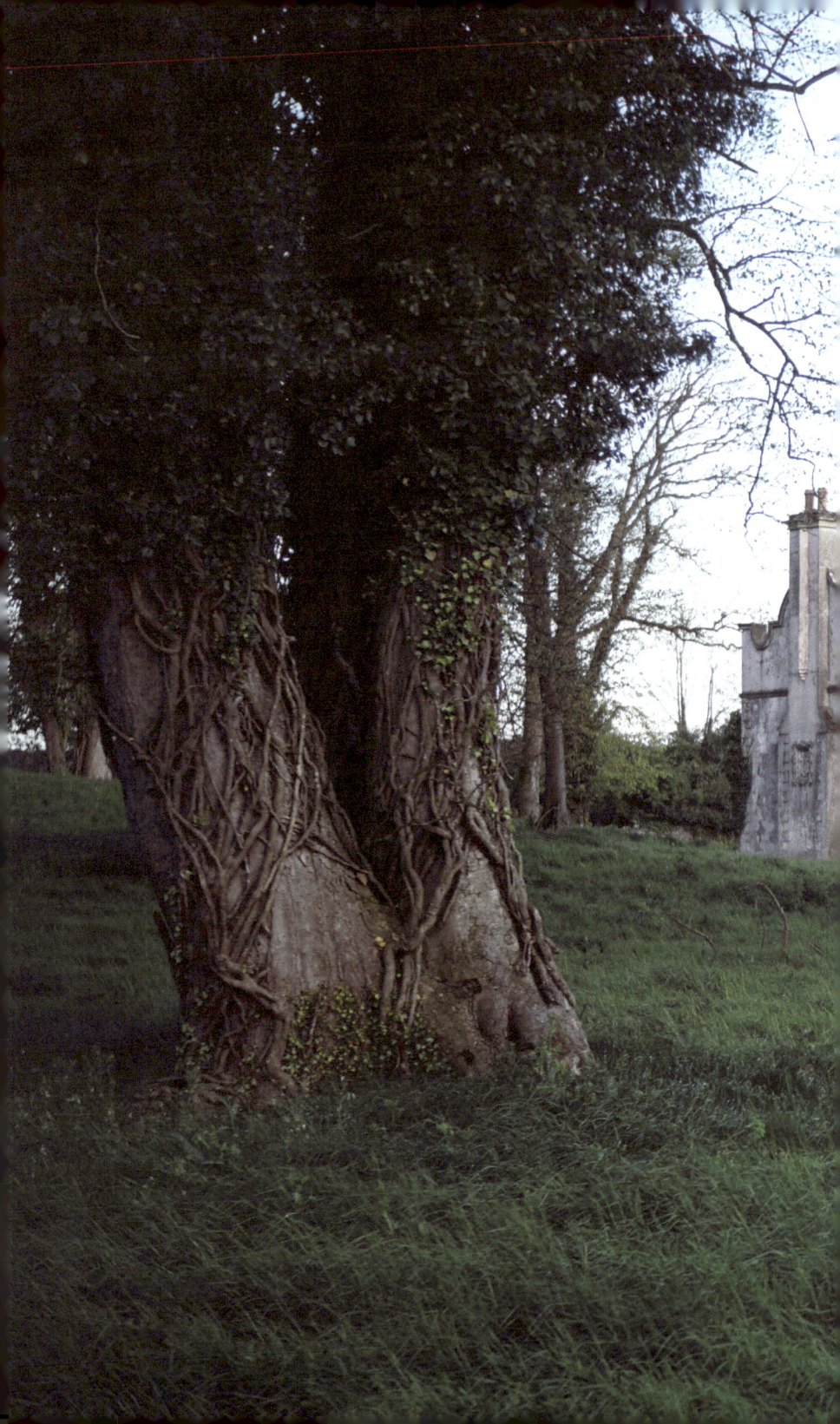

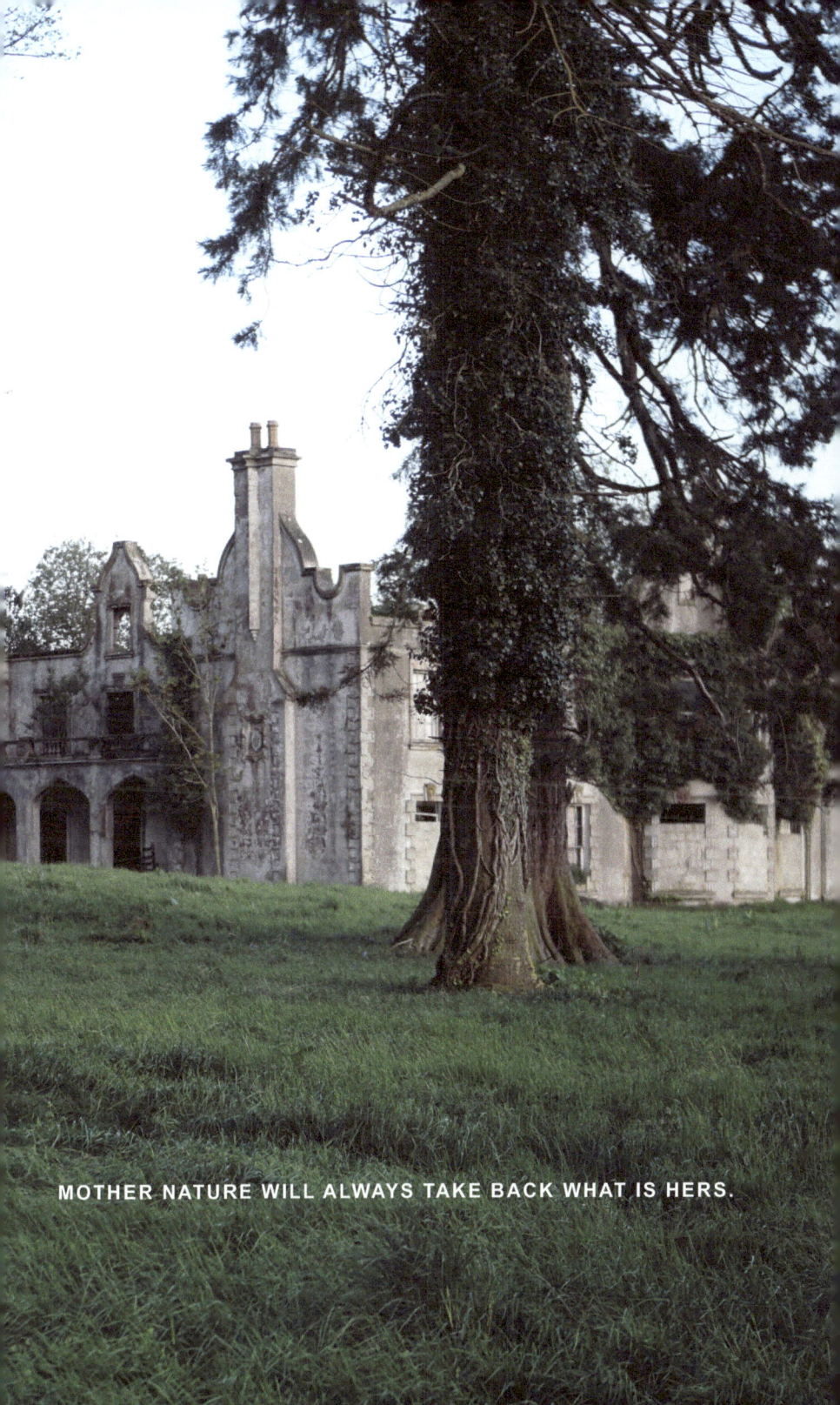

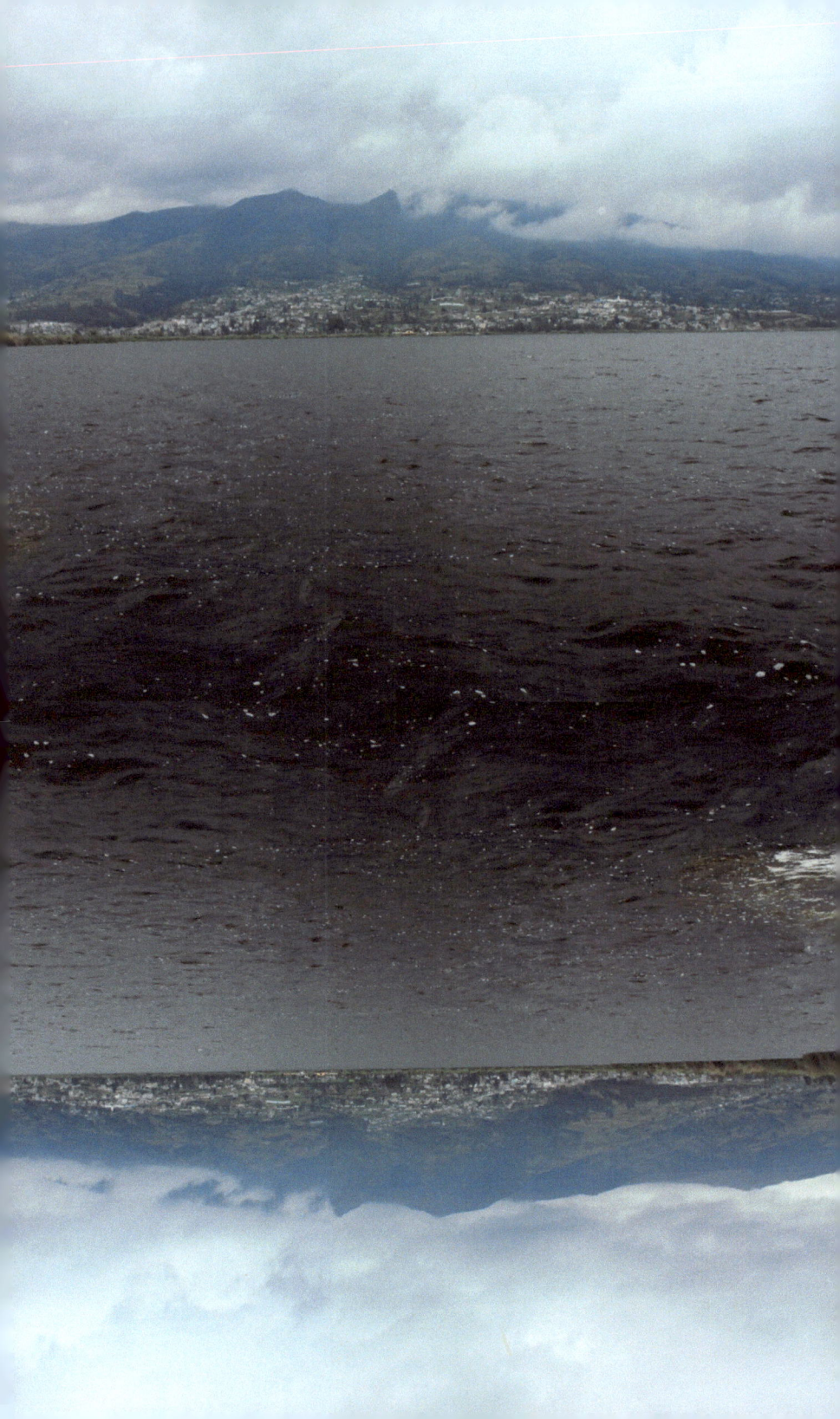

The Earth will not end with us.

Long after humankind has perished,
Mother Nature will persist valiantly.

Her glorious bounty encapsulates the essence of creation,
The most deleterious of forces are no match for her great strength.

She is the Alpha and the Omega,
From the first burst of light to Her final breath.

The Earth will not end with us.

REBEKAH C. GUERRA

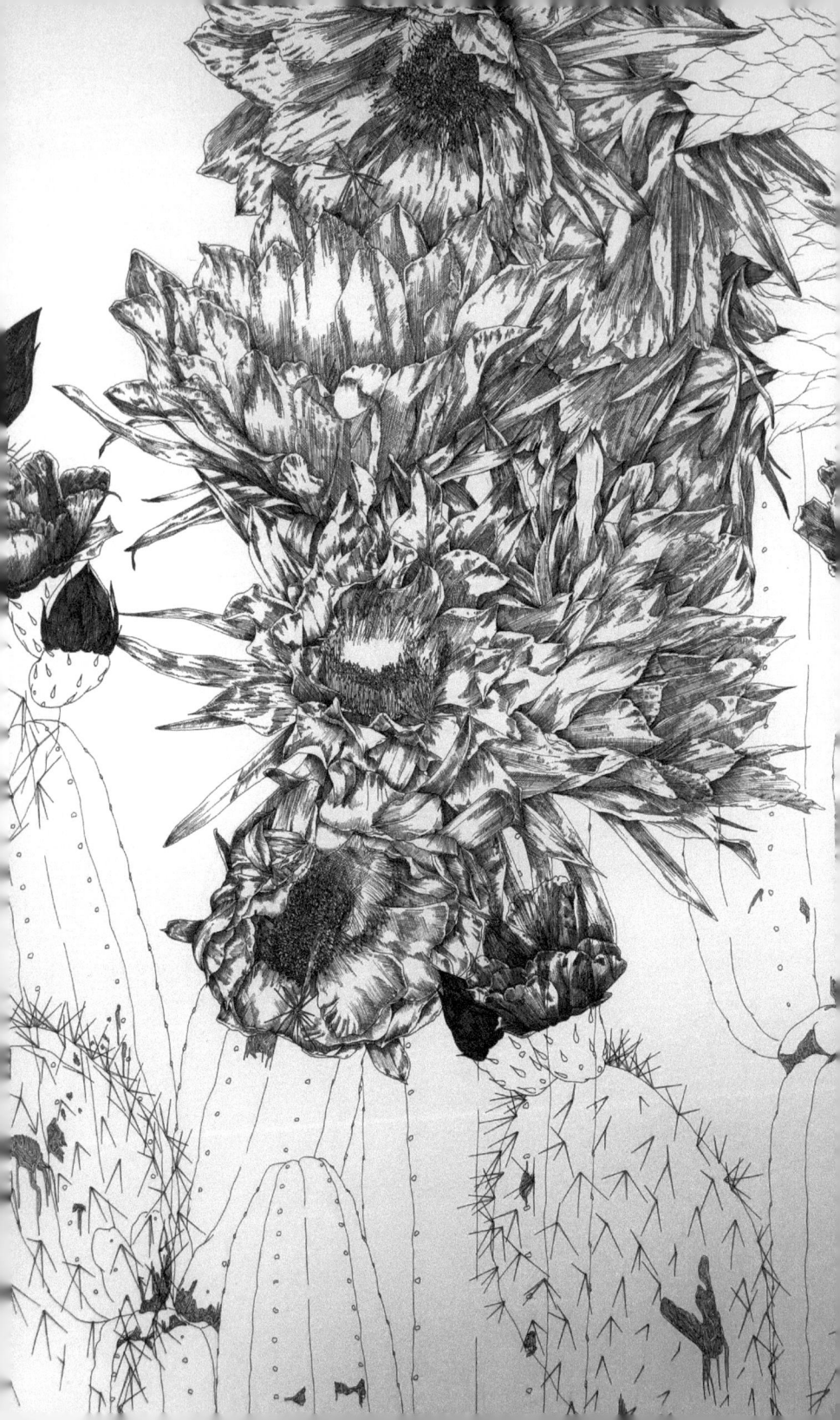

First came summer.
Our bodies dripping sweat
In the heat of our love,
As we swore in our hearts
We would shine for a lifetime.

Then came fall
The colors were changing
In parallel with your heart,
As I clutched and begged,
Watering you with tears.
But just as the trees
Are powerless over their leaves,
You were gone by November.

Then came winter.
The snow providing
an illusion of a new slate
only to leave me frozen in time
to every memory of your touch.

But you found shelter.
You were able to create
a facade of summer in her arms,
While I faced the howl
Of my wolves at night.

And now...spring
My soul is ready to bloom.
But my heart is left timid.
I withstood the winter
and faced my demons,
But I am too scared
to step into the sun and thaw.

It is only now that I can look
to the trees and flowers
in sacred reverence.
For they
have the courage to bloom,
year after year,
Only to face yet another
fall and winter.

<yarrow>

Illustration *by Carri*

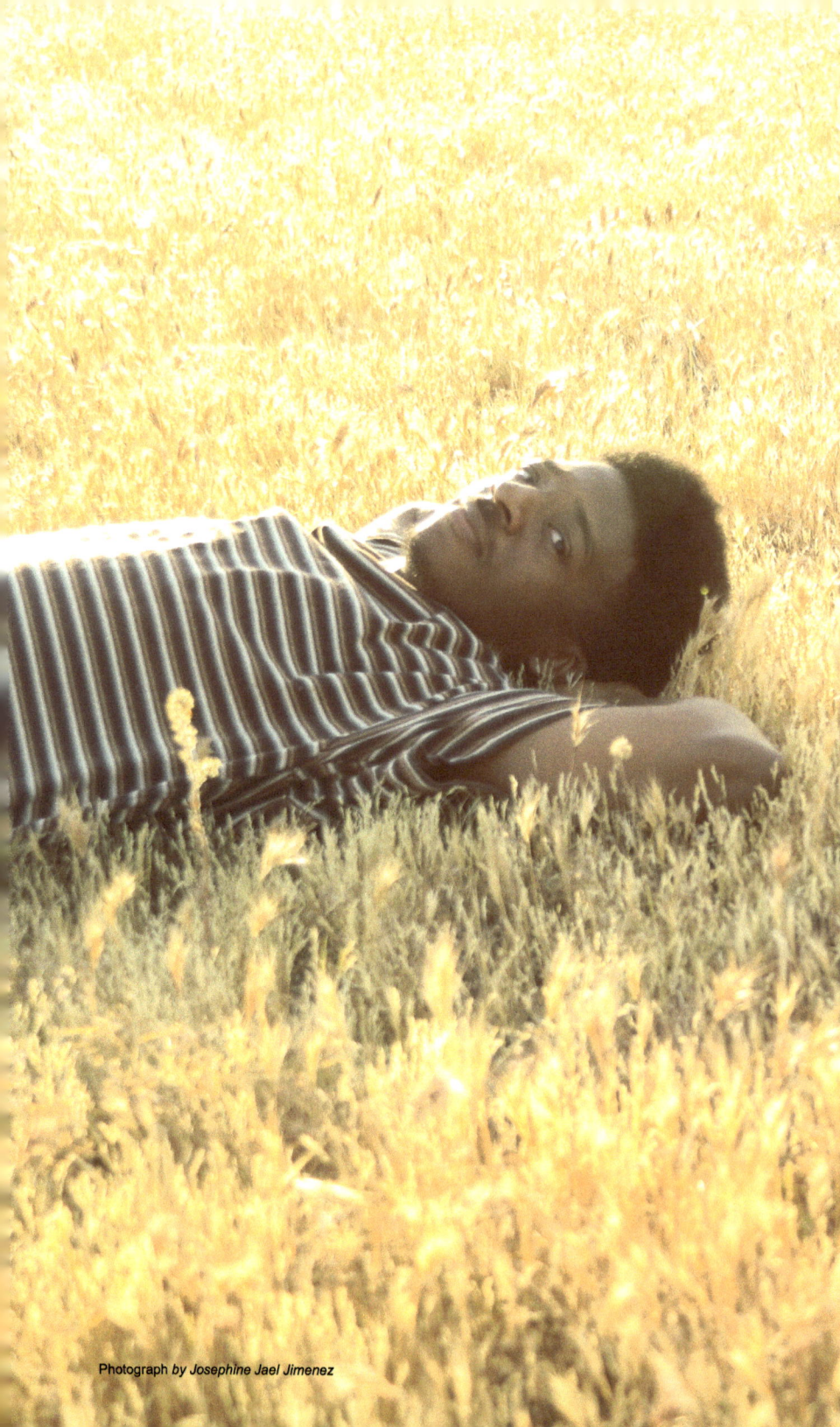

Photograph by Josephine Jael Jimenez

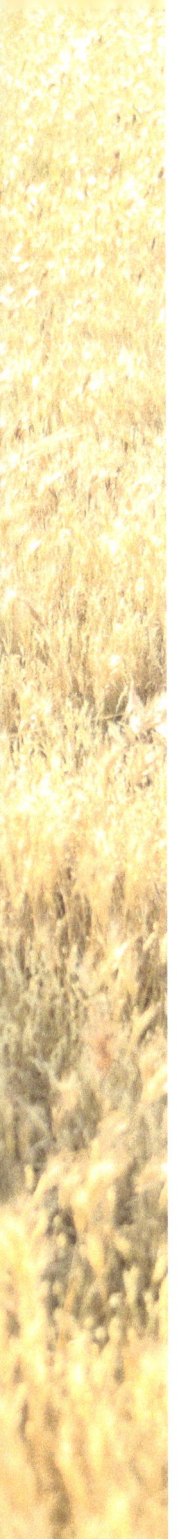

ME, WE, AND THE BEES

JOSEPHINE JAEL JIMENEZ

There are bees falling from the sky. Well, they're falling out of the bathroom vent. Close enough.

Sometimes they fall with death already over them, but sometimes they fall with their wings still buzzing them across the floor. They hold on to life more fervently than anyone or anything I have ever seen. The amount of energy they're mustering up just to die faintly in the background would probably be too much for us brittle humans, proportionately that is.

When I wake up in the morning and head to the bathroom, I have to look where I step. Can bees still sting you once they're dead? Even if they can't, I feel a deep respect for these little creatures and would never be able to forgive myself if I were to step on their corpses. They fought too hard for their teaspoon of honey. I feel guilty for being part of the species that steals it from them.

The exterminator came and placed poison in our vents. "They'll be dead in 72 hours," he said. Nothing to worry about. They were just looking for somewhere to build a hive. They were just trying to build a life.

After the exterminator came, they fell more frequently. Aren't bees in danger of dying? Aren't we in danger of dying if they're in danger of dying? There should be a sense of guilt when you feel as if you're contributing to the demise of the human race, but that doesn't come to me.

We cheat, we steal, we murder. Humans have ruined everything because we wanted everything to belong to us. We fell in lust with the things that were placed in our view and we lie to our souls and say it's love. But love doesn't cheat, or steal, or murder. Love doesn't result from those, either. Humans are lust and maybe we deserve to be extinct.

But not these bees. I should have left them to fall naturally from the sky. One or two wouldn't have been the end of the world. Daily burials wouldn't have killed me. But this steady stream of bodies floating down from the ceiling just might. I have no regrets.

A LAZY PERSON'S GUIDE TO SAVING THE WORLD

Don't know the reasons why?
Well I'm not a fucking computer,
Google it.

RIDE A FUCKING BIKE OR TAKE A FUCKING WALK. STOP KILLING TURTLES, BUY A METAL STRAW. SINGLE USE PLASTIC IS FOR LOSERS, SKIP THE WATER BOTTLES. YOU'RE NOT GONNA WEAR THAT THREE YEARS FROM NOW, DITCH FAST FASHION.

DISPOSE OF ALL YOUR ECLECTRONIC JUNK THE RIGHT WAY, DUH. YOUR CHEMICALS ARE KILLING YOU, MAKE YOUR OWN CLEANING PRODUCTS. FINALLY STEP FOOT IN A FUCKING LIBRARY. YOU REALLY DON'T NEED THAT MUCH MAKEUP.

EAT LESS MEAT. VOTE WITH YOUR WALLET. LEARN HOW TO FUCKING COMPOST. WASH YOUR CLOTHES IN COLD WATER, IT WON'T KILL YOU. TURN. OFF. THE. FUCKING. LIGHTS. COOLING AND HEATING ALL YEAR LONG IS STUPID.

GET OUT OF BED AND GO TO THE FARMER'S MARKET. TURN YOUR COMPUTER ALL THE WAY OFF, BETTER YET, USE IT LESS OFTEN. LINE DRY YOUR CLOTHES LIKE A REAL ADULT. UNPLUG THE THINGS YOU'RE NOT USING YOU MONSTER.

IF YOU'VE GOT A BABY, DEAL WITH THEIR SHIT AND BUY CLOTH DIAPERS. GET OVER YOURSELF AND USE A MENSTRUAL CUP. DITCH THE PAPER TOWELS AND NAPKINS ALREADY! VISIT YOUR LOCAL THRIFT STORE, YOU'LL LOOK GOOD FOR ONCE.

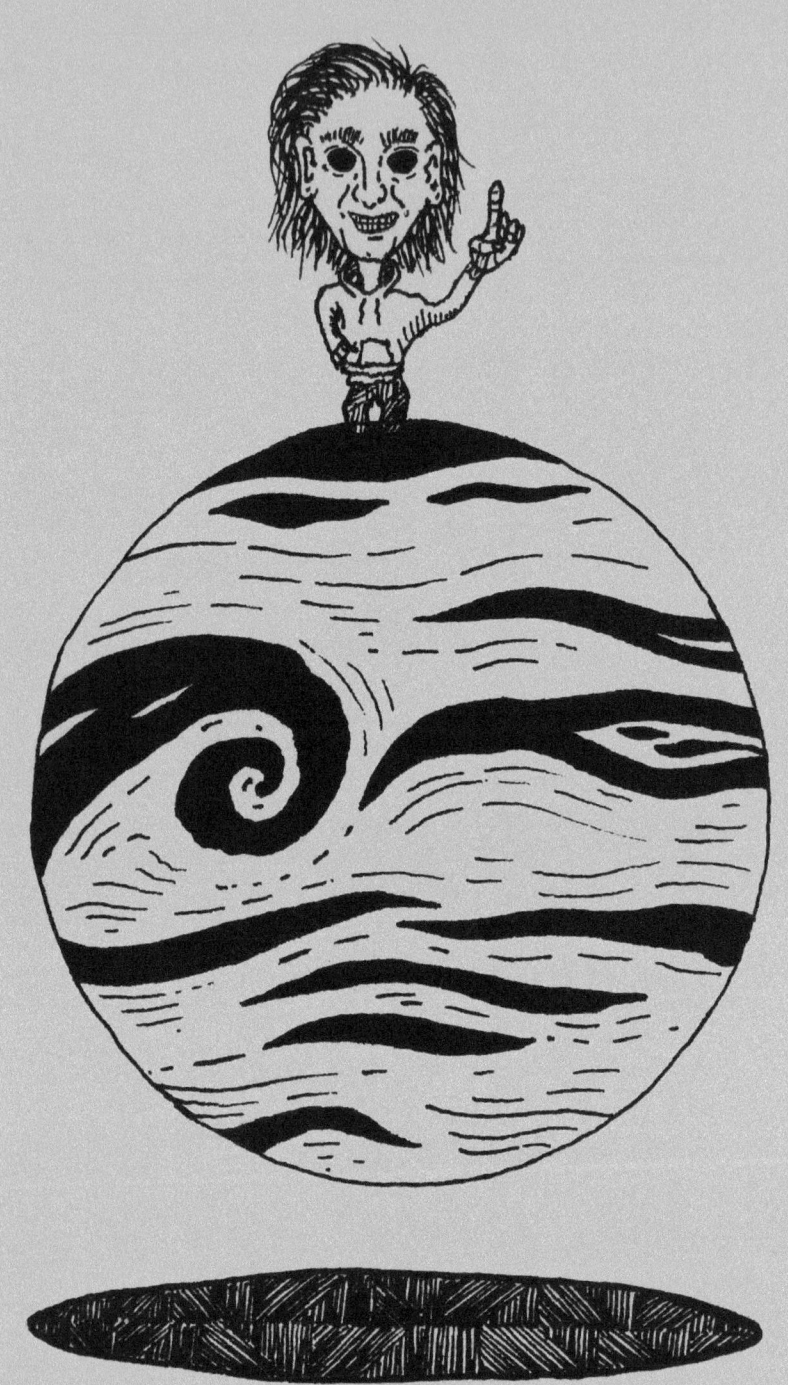

UNCONDITIONAL LOVE
MELISSA ARELLANO

We take and take, yet you keep on giving.
We've ripped your hair up by the roots
We've suffocated you with cruel acrid smoke
We've ravished and molded your body.
We've polluted your oceans with remnants of our lives…
And yet, you keep on giving.

Yet there are times when you get angry.
You whip us with wind,
You howl into the cracks of our home
You moan
And cry,
Your desolate cry..
It reverberates through our homes
And chills us to the bone.
You drench us with torrential rains,
You create menacing,
Seemingly apocalyptic storms.
As if you're telling us, begging us
To slow down from our mundane lives
To look around,
And appreciate all that you've given us.

Thank you for the splendid sights
Thank you for those spectacular moments of awe
In your glory you are truly a sight to behold.

Illustration *by Shane Cronin*

MOTHER NATURE

ROBERTA FISHER

Oh mother,
Your nature is one of one,
No competition,
We feel your power through the sun.
Oh mother,
Forgive us for we have often misunderstood you,
Failed to acknowledge your hurt,
And often abused you.
Oh mother,
If we knew better, we would do better,
For you should be held and loved,
So loved that we warm you,
Change the view on global warming,
Like bumble bees, just swarm you.
Oh mother,
We adore you,
From the domestic familiarities all the way up to the foreign you.
Oh mother,
We adore you,
We love your nature,
How you nurture,
And we'll always be for you.

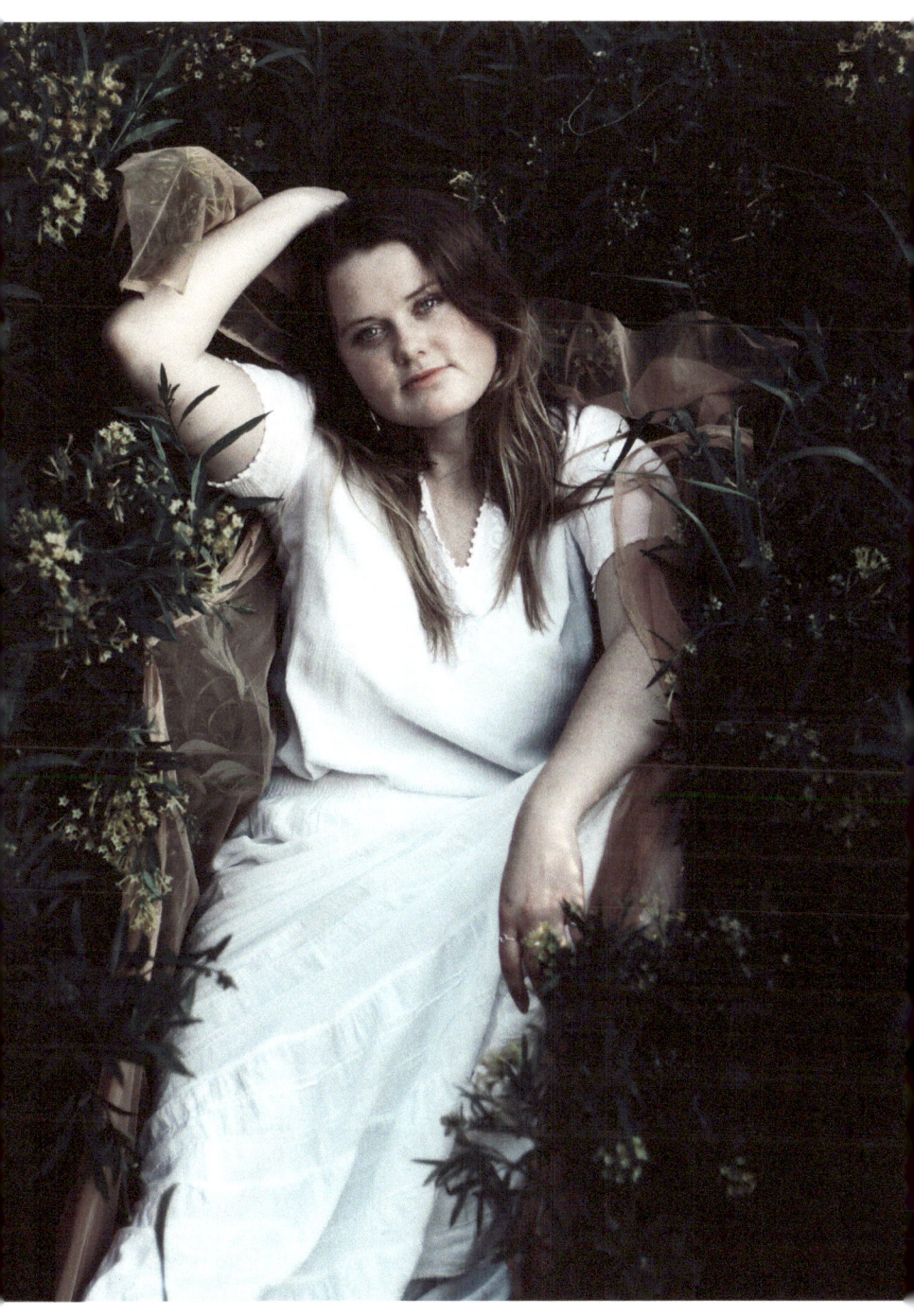

Unveiled. The Series
Photograph *by Pierre Van Vuuren*

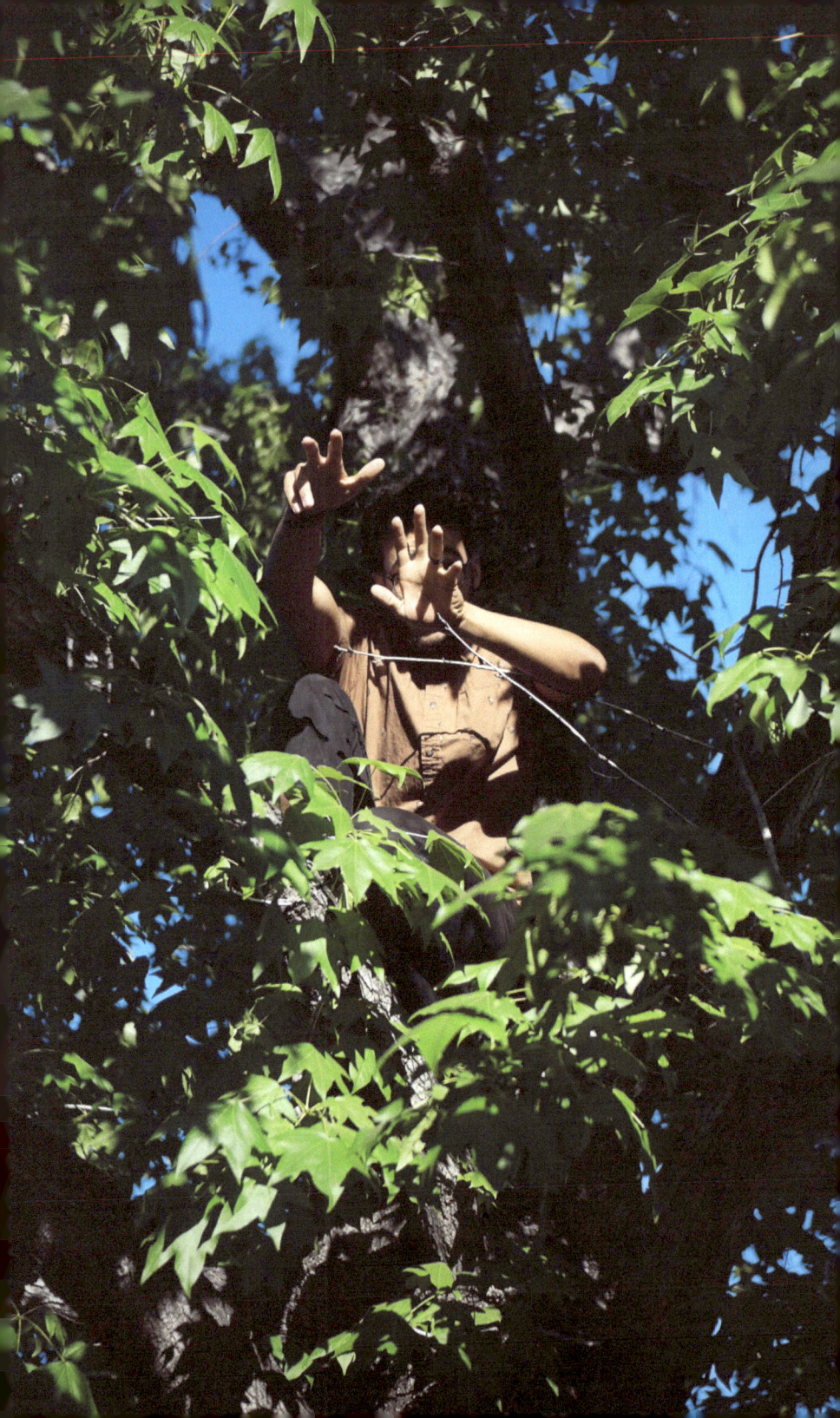

Coming up roses
when I wanted
was to be a weed,
rebelling against everyone
but mother earth.

Photography & Poem *by Josephine Jael Jimenez*

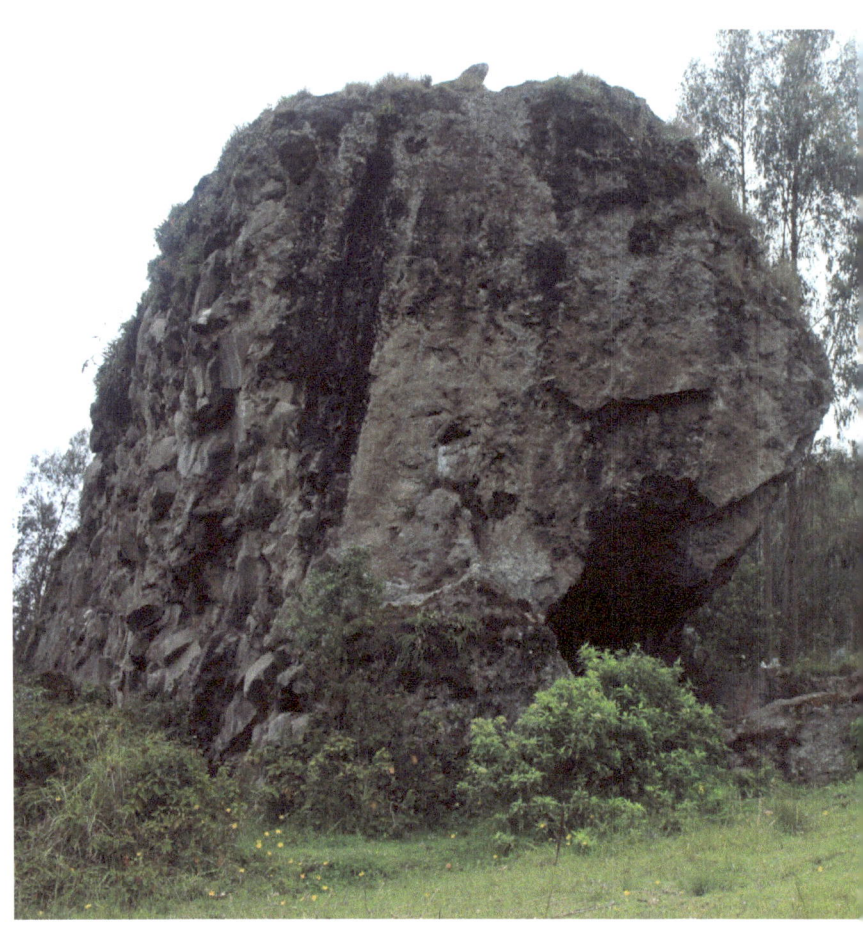

Photograph & Poem *by Yura Sapi*

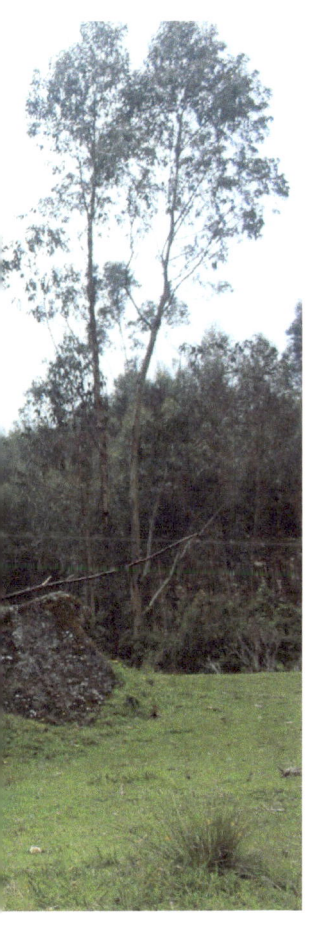

Piedra perdida
En medio de mamá y tayta

Piedra para las perdidas
En medio de un logro
a el próximo
En un juego de esperando
y esperanza

Piedra perdida
Nos encuentras en el momento
Que más te necesitamos

Piedra perdida
Nos encuentras
Y ya no estamos perdidas
Pay mil a la piedra perdida

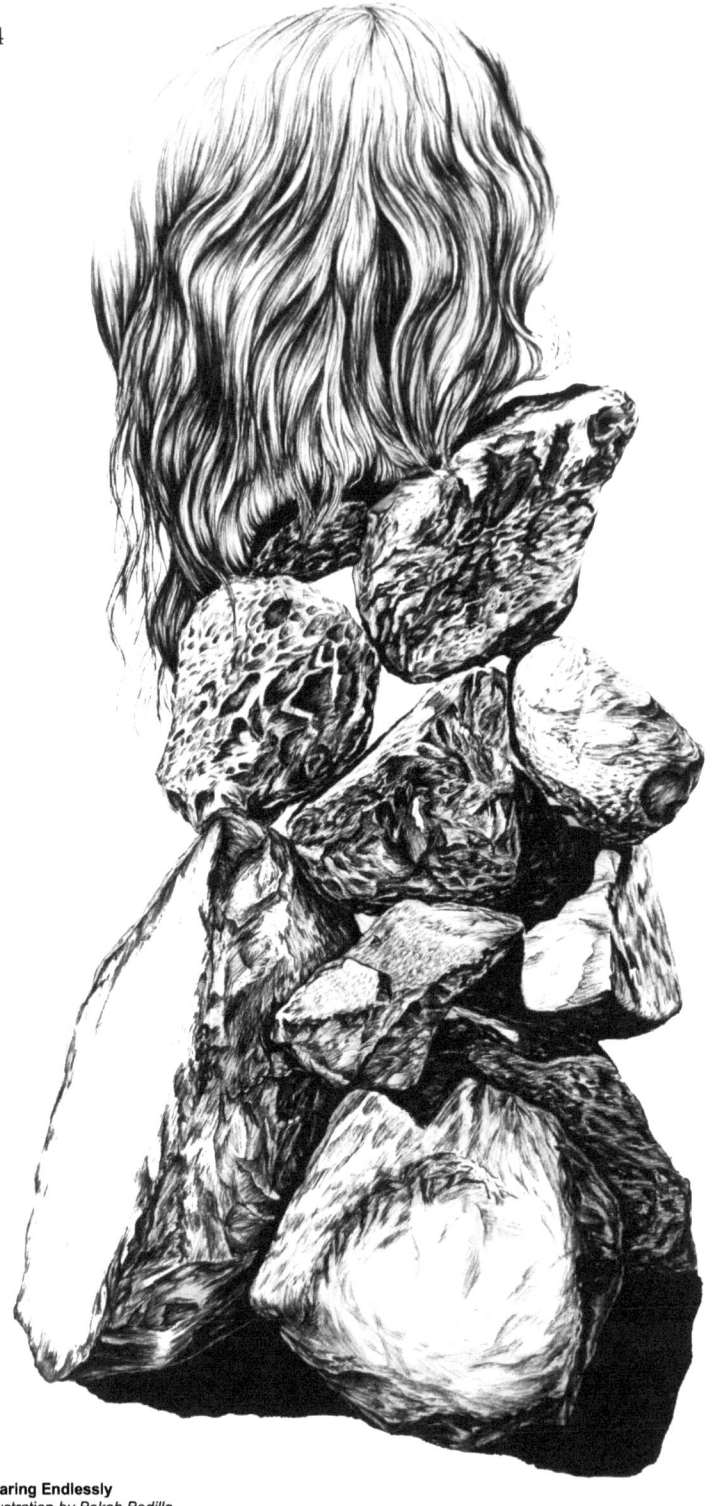

Staring Endlessly
Illustration *by Bekah Badilla*

PORTRAIT OF THE SALTON SEA
After Christopher Soto's "SELF PORTRAIT AS SONORAN DESERT"

MADELEINE SIMMONS

She walks across his chest—
                         dragging her tears & wounds
                               [filled with salt].
The desert blooms // into cracks—
             gases & flumes.

She takes it // shrinking one inch more.
   —for a second a sweet breeze picks her up.
Reminding her of happiness // once—
                      shared // like rain.
She was reminded because // the winds travel north.
[can winds relocate a sea?]
                    Where it once was a lake—
                        Named Maple like leaves.
[Coordinates— I carved in a bracelet].   Coordinates— my sister tattooed to her side.

She howls now
                    [As the desert // surrounds her].
She coughs &
shrinks // away from // his chest
             [filled with fear].
A stranded sea left in the desert —
                [She is labeled] "sick "wounded"
                    She sleeps in another room &
Mental health & her body are—
Her life —   was man [made].
Her life made //   by those who left her.

OUR PEOPLE

BEKAH BADILLA
@bekahbad
bekahbadilla.com

BRENDA HERNÁNDEZ JAIMES
@bren_jai
brenjai.com

CARRI
@carri_fernanda

JOSEPH A. REYES
@joeykangarooooo

JOSEPHINE JAEL JIMENEZ
@josietakestheworld
josietakestheworld.com

MADELINE SIMMONS
@madeleinemsimmons

MELISSA ARELLANO
@melsartpetals

PIERRE VAN VUUREN
@pierre.tography

ROBERTA FISHER
@msrobertafisher

REBEKAH C. GUERRA
rebekahguerra.com

SHANE CRONIN
@dope_ghost
dopeghost.squarespace.com

YARROW
@apoetandherpup

YURA SAPI
@vivforthemoment
@advancingartsforward

YOUNG IGNORANTES
@youngignorantes
youngignorantes.com

www.ingramcontent.com/pod-product-compliance
Lightning Source LLC
Chambersburg PA
CBHW040338220526
45473CB00009B/2731